THE POETRY GAMES: TRUTH OR DARE?

VERSES FROM THE
WEST MIDLANDS

Edited By Allie Jones

First published in Great Britain in 2018 by:

Young Writers
Remus House
Coltsfoot Drive
Peterborough
PE2 9BF
Telephone: 01733 890066
Website: www.youngwriters.co.uk

FOREWORD

Welcome to *The Poetry Games: Truth Or Dare? - Verses From The West Midlands.*

For this Young Writers poetry competition we encouraged self-expression from secondary school pupils through a truth or dare format. The 'truth' entries reveal what the writer is passionate about, offer a sincere expression of their emotions or share their hopes, dreams and ambitions. The 'dare' entries are provocative in order to question the conventional and voice the writer's opinion; they may fight for their beliefs in verse or just tell a poetic tale of an audacious adventure.

We encouraged the writers to think about the technical aspects of their poems' compositions, whether they be an acrostic, haiku, free verse or another form, and to consider techniques such as metaphors, onomatopoeia, rhyme and imagery.

I'm so impressed with both the content and the style of the poems we received and I hope you enjoy them as much as I have. I'd like to congratulate all the writers who entered this competition and took up the challenge to join Team Truth or Team Dare.

Enjoy!

CONTENTS

Finlay Chetwood (12)	76
Thomas Bratton (11)	77
Eloise Cox (12)	78
Paris Skye Callaway (12)	79
Charlotte Holbrook (12)	80
Gabriella Bickley (11)	81
Olivia Kessey (11)	82
Rebecca Gripton (13)	83
Prem Mehmi (11)	84
Morgan Groome (13)	85
Olivia May	86
Louis Mansell (12)	87
Harriet Bailey (12)	88
Freya Cox (12)	89
Stephanie Tomkinson (12)	90
Connor Lewis (11)	91
Amelia Reid-Mellor (13)	92
Chelsea Louise Davidson (11)	93
Molly Louise Leonard (13)	94
Kelly Alice Griffiths (12)	95
Emily Bullock (12)	96
Katie Jones (12)	97
Taran Kang (12)	98
Ruby Lily Gittins (12)	99
Tiah Summer Hunt (11)	100
Kane Jones (12)	101
Ben Yates-Ward (12)	102
Kyle Richardson (11)	103

King Edward's School, Birmingham

Harry Kite (13)	104

King's High School, Warwick

Eowyn Charman (12)	106
Aneeka Rai	109
Christabel Alun-Jones	110
Freya Richardson (11)	112
Katie Burrows (14)	114
Evie Madeleine Griffin (13)	116
Shivanshi Bhatt (13)	118
Hannah Broome (13)	120

Megan Galliford (11)	122
Qi Qi Xie (12)	124
Anoushka Mundey (14)	126
Anne Mynors	128
Catherine Reynolds (13)	130
Molly Charlotte McCusker (12)	132
Gracie Lloyd (12)	133
Rachel Eslick (13)	134
Amy Edwards (12)	136
Freya Laycock (13)	137
Nathania Adu-Boahen (13)	138
Olivia Pascoe (12) & Gemma W (12)	139
Jemima Hunt (12)	140
Charlotte Emily Rachel Perry (12)	141
Millie Perkins	142
Evie Jeavons	143
Olivia Smith (12)	144
Maddy Phillips (12)	145
Thuwaraha Viveananthan (13)	146

Kings Heath Boys' School, Kings Heath

Mudassar Hussain (12)	147
Harry Cleaver (12)	148
Yousef Atallah (16)	150
Muhammad Ali Gohir (12)	152
Muhammad Swara (14)	153

THE POEMS

MOTHER

Truth

When I was young, she would walk before me,
There to set an example and lead the way
If I should ever fall forward
She would catch me, and in her arms I would stay.

When I was a teen, she would walk behind me
To be there, should I ever require
If I was to make a single request
She would be present to fulfil my desire.

When I was an adult, she would walk beside me
So that as two friends, we could enjoy life together
Sharing memories and happy moments
Relying on each other forever and ever.

Of all the special joys in life
Including all large and small
A mother's love and tenderness
Is the greatest of them all.

Surayyah Amatul Aziz (15)
Bordesley Green Girls' School, Birmingham

AN UNEXPECTED REALITY

Dare

Time, people and laws have changed,
We will never go back, like this we'll stay.
Technology has upgraded, price tags have been raised,
Old times will never be seen again.

We wish tomorrow can bring what we lost yesterday,
Let it be exposed through the dew that takes its time to evaporate.

But the delightful memories we yearn for cannot blind us from the evil that has been replaced.
The tragedy we have adapted to has simply been accepted as part of fate.

Those in power stand like singular weeds amongst a perfect crop field.
It's astonishing how their indoctrination can infect something so beautiful.

I was warned about them in my bedtime story books,
The wolves from the fairy tale, 'Little Red Riding Hood'.

They attack indirectly, in the most innocent way,
They diminish our old memories and put new ones in place.

Children's minds are now corrupted with silly,
Irrelevant games.
The sun is waiting for them to come out and play.
Laughter and joy has faded away,
Everyone has parted following a path of their own taste.

The kind old day is left alone,
No more infants, they are absorbed in smartphones.
The pitter-patter of feet and chitter chatter of teens,
Has rotated to mumbling and silence in the streets.

No sign of happiness, where has it gone?
Thrown down the drain and no longer to be found.

People are drowning in the sea of gloom.
Never knew such a nightmare was ever to come true.

It is a time where we are getting pulled into the depths of
doom...
Please my friends, make sure it's not you.

Qudsiyah Zara Ahsan (17)
Bordesley Green Girls' School, Birmingham

THE SAVIOUR

Dare

Started fresh again like a leaf,
Known one day I will fall from failure,
Tried to keep up,
But the speed was too fast.
I needed a saviour,
To heal my pain,
She pulled me back to life again,
To see the world by how it truly is.

Thought what I could do,
Knowing I can fail every moment,
Being pushed down,
Onto the cold, hard floor,
No way to restart.

Hopes collapsed,
Dreams were the light,
Failing was the darkness,
Tried to survive,
Thought every moment,
That I could lose the fight,

Everyone tried to break me,
Wash away my colours
But I went higher
With the flow.

They don't know the feeling,
And they never will,
Making me think they are all around me,
Tried to leave me behind,
But they failed.

My saviour took me higher,
Knowing that slow and steady can win,
Dreams helped me,
Hope led my way.

I staggered behind,
But got help from friends and foe,
They gave me the flow,
And helped me carve my own path.
Knowing I am still carrying the burden.
From last year.

And the race is on,
Trying to eliminate all the players,
Leaving them weakened,
So they can be pushed around,
Like last year.

But this time,
I am going through the same thing,
But.. I hope... just hope,
Nothing happens to me,
Or the players.

But ...

I staggered behind,
But got help from friends and foe,
They gave me the flow,
And helped me carve my own path.
Knowing I am still carrying the burden.
From last year.

Ayesha Navid (12)
Bordesley Green Girls' School, Birmingham

UNTITLED

Truth

You will never be brave
If you don't get hurt
You will never learn
If you don't make mistakes
You will never be successful
If you don't encounter failure

Stars can't
Shine
Without darkness
So make
Them miss
The beautiful
Sun that
Makes
You smile.

Aqsa Khan (11)
Bordesley Green Girls' School, Birmingham

UNTITLED

Truth

If you want the truth
I will tell you the truth
Listen to the secret sound
The real sound
Which is inside you.

Iqra Ahmed (11)
Bordesley Green Girls' School, Birmingham

EHLERS-DANLOS SYNDROME AND ME

Truth

E verything hurts, the relenting pain never stops.

H ypermobility is everywhere in my body.

L oose joints, that don't stay put.

E xtreme fatigue, I just want to sleep.

R adiating pain from my head to my feet.

S ubluxations, which joints will be next?

D octors! I've lost count of the number I've seen.

A nd to top it all, I have brittle bones too.

N obody wanting to give me a hand.

L ack of understanding from people around.

O bvious difficulties that I have every day.

S how some support and ask if I'm okay.

S plints for my wobbly joints, crutches and a wheelchair.

Y ear after year, it seems to be getting worse.

N ormal, what's that? This is my normal.

D islocating every day, it does get in the way.

R outine of physio, at least twice a day.

O utstanding consultant who gives me fantastic care.

M edications that make me feel like a walking pharmacy.

E verything hurts, the relenting pain never stops.

Hannah Blaxall (13)

Burton Borough School, Newport

RESULTS OF BULLYING

Dare

(Dedicated to the memory of my friend)

Think of yourself
lonely in your bed
You're hanging swinging
from a golden thread.

Empty, alone
With the monsters within,
Eternally screaming,
You just want to give in.

Imagine that's you
Every day, every hour.
Forever sinking like
A withering flower.

You try to tell your dad
You try to tell your mum.
But they say you're being silly,
You're just got to move on.
You're just looking for attention, right?

You think there's no one
Who knows how you feel

You're just so alone,
But the feelings they're real.

Useless, neglected, forgotten, distressed
Alone, afraid but most depressed
And your friends go on
Like nothing's changed.

They must not care
The thoughts whisper
The lies in your brain.

You can't escape it
Trapped in your own skin.
You're ugly, you're hated
But you hide it with a grin.

You hate what you feel
So instead you feel nothing
Your insides are numb
Your confidence crumbling.

You look to the other things
To stop the pain.
Cutting, pills, but it gives you no gain.

And the people around you
Shout abuse your way
'You're hurting yourself, stop it'
That's what they all say.

No matter how they plead
That you're broken inside,
They turn the other way,
They run, they hide.

They say you're just foolish,
It's all in your head
But when they realise,
What they've done
You're dead!

Kinga Stachowicz (12) & Ellie
Burton Borough School, Newport

WWII

Truth

Running, hiding,
Taking cover
As the enemy planes approached
Cowering as the droning grew louder
And destruction followed in their wake.

The front line is a dangerous place
As bronze shells whizzed past your head
As my life turned upside down,
As the life of my comrades were snatched away
And as I saw my best friend fall.

I was filled with a volcanic rage.
As I drove my bayonet into the enemy's chest,
And as I ran and ducked for cover.
I saw the faces of all the men I killed
A bronze shell flew at my face,
I always knew my time would come
For karma to catch up with me.

As sadness filled my family and friends.
I shall always be with them.

Josh Mansell (12)
Burton Borough School, Newport

13

SPEAK

Truth

In a time that I tried to forget,
When I felt no comfort,
I was silent, a library.

Full of thoughts that I ached to say,
Did not because of fear of harsh repercussions.
Fearful of how people would judge me.
Even get teased or bullied
Prefer to stay silent I convinced myself
Then no ammunition was there.

Deeper I dug, the more I refused to move
'Speak, speak, talk, talk,' they said
Burying myself I ignored;
They would not like me, alone I would be
Speak, speak, no, no.

Misery enclosed my heart
The situation was twisted
People liked me, were friendly even if I didn't speak
Still I clung, too dangerous I can risk
Talk, talk, no, no.

Boomerangs seemed to twist inside my head
I came up with responses in class
Some did not think so,

I didn't think if I didn't speak.
Not all had that opinion I learnt
Like a bunch of hens taking a chick under its wings
Subtle encouragement and kindness flowed
It had been there all along I realised,
For the first time my confidence glowed
Speak, speak, yes I did!

Eve Hutchinson (13)
Burton Borough School, Newport

KARMA

Dare

On the corner of the street,
Abandoned and dirty,
You sit there.
Now aged thirty.

A spark of recognition
Flashes through my mind.
I know you from before,
A past I left behind.

Tears sting my eyes,
I know you were the one,
To abuse me every day,
When all my hope was gone.

Way back then,
You thought you were so cool
Head held high, stone-cold eyes,
The ultimate king of high school.

I was your target right?
Just a weak little girl,
A peasant among nobles,
A speck of dirt among pearl.

You obviously didn't care,
When I went home crying every night,
Just to be a burden to my parents,
A dull candle with a fading light.

But I see you here now,
I walk by, try to hold back a grin,
As they say what goes around comes around,
And karma's had another win.

But as I walk I stop,
Should I help?
Should I feel bad?
But every memory of you,
Just makes me feel mad...

Tia Ward (13)
Burton Borough School, Newport

MY DOG

Truth

Dogs are just one of those things, that come and go.
But not for me.
Happiness, dreamy, love when you collect them from their mum.
All the puppy training, teething and certainly mischievious things.
But you just don't think about... it!

Until they get old and all the trips to the vets and it's that little face,
Almost even cuter than a puppy.

Then, the day the vets come, it's like they take your dog, you cry and you cry.
You just don't realise!
Then they're gone!

All the pain, gone!
They are free, more free than ever before.
It's like a pot of gold and the end of the rainbow.
But you really miss them!
Then the day you become old, gone!

The eyes, then the ears and the whiskers,
They all go up.
Then, you finally reunite. The lick of the face
and the smell, oh the smell.

I know all this,
Because it happened to me and I will see him again.

Beth Norton Wyre (12)
Burton Borough School, Newport

I'M JUST A DOG IN A CRAZY MAN'S WORLD

Dare

Here I am, all alone,
Just wanting to play,
But that's not safe,
I was taken from home.

No one understands my pain, my fear,
Though I wish to have fun,
I worry when they at last come,
For they abuse me until I follow.

I wish I had a loving family,
To take me to their home,
I feel sad and alone,
Until I am there.

The lights make me blind,
The words that they shout,
Eat me alive,
Please help me!

I have to fight,
Fight for my life,
Against my family, my friends,
Please save me!

Every night I pray,
For my voice to be heard,
And all to be over,
Once and for all,

I just long to be free,
But no one hears my cries,
I mean after all...
I'm just a dog in a crazy man's world.

Evie Violet Youens (12)
Burton Borough School, Newport

TRUTH OR DARE?

Dare

Truth and dare
Two different things
Both seem so shallow
Yet have more meaning.

They say dare is more dangerous
But it's the truth that corrupts
So the truth is worse?
But it's dare that self-destructs.

The intentions of everyone
A truth that can't be revealed
Find the secrets of society
A dare to keep sealed.

Dare, climb a mountain
Truth, why is it there?
A few know the answer
Others just don't care.

The ones that found the dare
And the ones that know the truth
All the secrets I'm built on
And all the world's lies too.

So if you want to lose your sanity
If you want to destroy your youth
I'll show you the truth of the dare.
If you dare to find the truth.

Hattie Mitchell (13)
Burton Borough School, Newport

I BELIEVE

Dare

I believe we all have different journeys,
I believe everyone can follow their dreams
I believe everyone can look up not down
I believe life is a opportunity
I believe you should look forward not back.

I believe life is a struggle, fight it
I believe life is full of fun
I believe life is a camera, just focus on what's important.
I believe there is no word 'can't'.

I believe life is a promise, fulfil it
I believe life is luck, make it
I believe life is everything
I believe you can do anything if you believe.

I believe life is a duty, complete it.
I believe life is an adventure, dare it
I believe life is too short to be someone else.

Grace Beardmore (11)
Burton Borough School, Newport

THE BENCH OF TEARS

Truth

Take me to the meadows
Take me to the sweet-smelling blossom tree.
I want to escape this chamber cell
I want to ring the finish bell.

When will the emperor of names stop?
I'm only a small kid
Help! I scream every day in my soul
Help! yells my mind.

Why me? Quaking my hands
Am I not like everyone else?
Why me? Cowering to life
Do I not speak the same language?
Do you not hear me scream?

The bench of tears is the only place I know
I don't know where to go.
She sees me sitting all alone
She sees my tears of sorrow,
And helps me dream my last dream.
Before I say hello to
The meadow of dreams.

Bethan Neal (13)
Burton Borough School, Newport

A TRUE FRIEND

Truth

I got put in here,
They cut off my ear,
And I don't know why?
It's just my sibling and I.

Every day I feel like the walls are caving in,
At least I got saved from my neighbours' bin,
In front of me, little mice are scurrying around,
I'm surprised that they're not afraid of the hound.

Strange noises are ringing through my ear,
Again I ask myself, why am I here?

Just as I was giving up,
I saw a family walking in looking for a pup.
They came up to my cage,
All happy and not in a rage.

Now I have a new home,
All clean and bright.
What true friends they really are.

Kathryn Charles (14)
Burton Borough School, Newport

THE WIND

Truth

Oh wind, you dance and move in many ways,
You tightly grasp the leaves and send them high,
They dance so freely through the trees that sway,
Fly rhythmically descending from the sky.
Your clutching strength can change from night to day,
When raging storms come churning like the sea,
You move and rearrange the scene your way,
And come and go through seasons as you please.
You build, create and sculpt the lounging dunes,
And carve the windblown gorse across the bay,
Destroying countless cities with monsoons,
Your forceful strength can blow the blue away.
But wind, you are my saviour and my friend,
Your gentle whisper must not ever end.

Freya Llewellyn-Smith (13)
Burton Borough School, Newport

EARTH - THE WAR PLANET

Dare

The blood on our hands,
The sea turns red,
Filled with blood, innocent civilians.
We stand there, we stand there
Debating, debating about what to do next,
Is this right?

Why do we do this?
Why is our world like this?
Troops storming into people's homes,
Innocent people getting their homes taken away.

Children fleeing, fleeing for safety.
The parents passing their children
To the front of the line,
To maybe help the children have a glimpse of hope.
And what for, to get more land?
To become wealthier?
Our world is broken and we need to do something fast,
Very fast.

Alexander Porello (12)
Burton Borough School, Newport

MEMORIES

Dare

They say we keep our memories forever,
But is this true,
When will we know?
The answer is never.

They go through our mind,
Day in and day out.
Whether it's a day at the beach,
Or a day at the park.
Or when our parents have had to shout.

They can change our emotions,
They can make us sad,
Make us cry,
Make us smile,
Make us giggle about memories of Grandad.

Whether it's a funny memory of eating too much pie
A sunset sky or of something that made you cry.
I hope to keep my memories until I die.

Sophie Elizabeth Leigh (13)
Burton Borough School, Newport

WHAT IS LIFE?

Truth

Life,
Is it a dream?
Is it real or fake?
Will we ever know?
You wake up and brush your teeth
And yet you still think
What is life?

You head to school,
You meet your friends
Yet, they don't act nice towards you
And then you think.
What is life?

As you head home and have your dinner
And you wait for your mum to come back
You think, *what is life?*
Is it real or is it fake?
Maybe it's just a dream?
As you think more about life you realise,
Life is everything.

Valdis Viksne (13)
Burton Borough School, Newport

REALITY

Truth

Fun and upbeat.
Hyper and smiley.
I may seem happy,
But everything around me is dying.
The trees fall down,
The plants wither away,
And the world gets warmer every day.
I slowly crumble, along with the world.
I wish I was just an ordinary girl.
My imagination takes control,
I'm no longer in reality.
My brain has saved me from being a casualty.
I'm on cloud nine.
I'm safe and sound.
But then I fall and hit the ground.
The ground is reality and I can't get up.
I'm slowly failing.
I'm giving up.

Gabrielle Edwards (14)
Burton Borough School, Newport

SURVIVOR

Truth

Four friends are in a field,
All are tired from playing,
No time for escaping,
The wrong time is coming,
My dad's heart is racing,
You may do some explaining,
Everyone is screaming,
Your heart is palpitating,
One black gun,
He falls down on,
His friend apologises,
But there is no going back,
It's done!
Maybe he's okay,
Maybe he's gone,
But thirty-five years later,
He's alive,
He won!
And now I'm twelve,
Nearly thirteen,
And my dad is the best dad you have ever seen!

Rebecca Stone (12)
Burton Borough School, Newport

WORLD AT WAR

Truth

Bang! The gunshots have started,
As a bullet ricochets off my helmet,
I screamed in total shock,
It was the most shocking thing I'd ever witnessed

Slush, slush, every step was in pain
In the muddy trenches it was a game.
It was hard to sleep,
And I only had to look around,
And it made me weep.

Hiss! I could smell smoke,
It made me cough and choke.
I thought, *quick shout for help,*
But it was no use I would just have to sit there
And let it just end in a yelp!

Luke Talbot (12)
Burton Borough School, Newport

ME

Truth

I could, but I'm not going to,
I'm never going to!
No one can make me
Or tell me who I need to be.

I was made to be who I am
Instagram can't mould me.
Snapchat can't shape me.
Only I chose who I will and want to be.

I can't be shown,
I won't be shown,
I dress how I want to dress.
I wear my hair how I want to wear my hair.

I could but I'm not going to
I'm never going to
No one can make me.
Or tell me who I want to be.
I am me!

Lucy Scott (13)
Burton Borough School, Newport

DON'T WORRY ABOUT IT

Truth

Don't worry about what they say,
It could be rivalries with teachers,
It could be about how much someone weighs,
It could be about someone's ugly features,
But most of the time,
It's about you.

'He doesn't belong in our group,'
'What is he doing here?'
'I could knock him out in one swoop.'
'Yo! I bet he's queer!'

When you walk over to them,
You hear little snippets,
When you ask them they say,
'Don't worry about it.'

Oliver Robinson (13)
Burton Borough School, Newport

FIRST DAY OF SCHOOL

Truth

You walk through the gates
Where schoolwork awaits
You can smell school food
But it doesn't pick up your mood.
First lesson good,
Second lesson is worse
Third lesson is PE and you're covered in mud
Fourth is where you're counting your purse
Lunch is here!
So refuel your energy.
Fifth has ended and you are smiling with glee.
With a dash to the bus stop
And run all the way home
You get undressed and shout, 'Oh my!'
This is when you have realised you have lost your school tie.

Thomas Steel (12)
Burton Borough School, Newport

JUDGING

Dare

As Einstein once said,
'If you judge a fish by its ability to climb a tree,
It will live its whole life believing it is stupid'.
Teachers are proud how you judge kids with target grades.
Are you proud how you haven't changed,
As much as cars have since the 1850s.
I just want to say, that Denmark and other places,
Are already making the school days shorter
And also abolished homework.
Even though kids only make a couple of percentages
Of our current population,
They are a hundred percent of our future.

Freddie Roberts (12)
Burton Borough School, Newport

DANCING TO THE GROUND

Truth

Dancing to the ground,
Turning red, yellow and brown,
Falling to the floor as it did.
Falling as a feather should.

Turning from green to brown
Summer dying down
Crushing as we go,
Sticking to our feet as we walk.

Cracking as we take a step at a time,
Jumping in, no care in the world.

The morning mist,
And the dew-spectacled grass
It made me feel bliss.

The dew on the grass,
The squirrels frantically bury nuts
Winter is due.
Autumn.

Ellie Meredith (12)
Burton Borough School, Newport

38

UNTITLED

Truth

I get used every day,
I get worn and battered.
She hurts my soul when she jumps,
Damaging the leather.
All I want is a day of rest,
But, night is all I get.
Here in the box, till morning comes
then the torture comes again.

Help me please,
I feel so isolated in this world.
All I need is a little freedom,
And a break to feel alive.

I've been cleaned and passed down,
To families and friends.
Either stuffed in a box or jumped on.
I never stop. I want to feel free.

Ruby Carrick (13)
Burton Borough School, Newport

WHAT IS BULLYING?

Truth

B is for bully, the horrid word that should never exist.

U is for upset because we all have feelings

L is for lonely because people do feel this

L is for love because everyone should feel loved.

Y is for you because it could happen to you.

I is for inside because inside people have feelings

N is for no because no one should be bullied

G is for go and talk to someone.

Bullying is a cruel thing and everyone should be helped and cared for!

Libby Anslow (12)
Burton Borough School, Newport

ANIMALS

Dare

Animals come,
Animals go,
But why?

Sea creatures come,
Sea creatures go,
But why?

Land animals come
Land animals go,
But why?

We hunt them down,
We kill them off,
We take their furs,
We take their skins,
We take their lives!
But why?

Is there any need for this cruelty,
Is there any need for this disgust,
Is there any need for this at all?

Animals come,
Animals go,
But why?

Brandon Luke (11)
Burton Borough School, Newport

UNFAIRNESS

Truth

U nder my sheets at night, thinking and thinking.

N ever going to do it, but I could try

F inally made it and decided to join.

A nd I made the right decision

I stand up there proud until something happens

R aging about it as I can't stop

N obody should choose under their ability

E veryone is equal

S ome people can be very picky

S ometimes the best people who stay are the ones who reach the stars! Everyone can do this!

Ella Majhu (12)
Burton Borough School, Newport

WHO ARE YOU?

Truth

Do you know who you are?
Is this person all just a vision from the stars?
Or do you deeply know who you are?
People all around you, changing all the time.
You may feel lonely, or just crowded by the fame.
You may feel low, no greater than a dime,
Always feeling sad, depressed or lame.
But is this person truly who you are?
Are you real, or just a devastation?
Next time you're alone, sitting afar,
Ask yourself,
Am I just a part of this fake civilisation?

Jessica Payne (13)
Burton Borough School, Newport

ICE SKATING

Truth

Forwards, backwards, carving letters
With my blades.
The cold on my face gets fresher each day.
Falling on my knees, bruises appear,
Training isn't easy, need to go in with no fear.
One... Two... Three... This jump I want to land,
But each time I try, it's like walking through no-man's-land.
One last try before I move on.
With determination and grit.
One more to tick off my list.
Yay, thank goodness my list is complete,
Now I can go and have a big feast.

Ella May Wood (12)
Burton Borough School, Newport

PAIN!

Truth

I am standing on the court, on the court,
Green bib on as I fought, as I fought.

I fall on the floor in pain, in pain,
Lying on the floor in the rain, in the rain.

I try to get up and stand, and stand,
Try to walk on the land, on the land.

I have to miss the next round, the next round,
Standing on the side getting drowned, getting drowned.

The rain is pouring heavy on us, on us,
I'm trying not to make a fuss, make a fuss.

Emma Fletcher (12)
Burton Borough School, Newport

THEY ARE YOUR DOGS

Dare

They are your friends
They are your soulmate
They are your defender
They are your date.

They are yours.

They love that you are funny
They love that you are stupid
They love you when they have a full tummy.
But even more when you are deluded.

They are yours

You love it when they chase from one end to another
They act as a sibling to you, a sister or a brother.

They are yours
They are your dogs.

Hannah Ash (12)
Burton Borough School, Newport

SCHOOL WARS

Dare

Conflict in a school
How can this be?
A place with rules
Where kids are let free
Gangs around a school
Of children nonetheless
With teachers acting like fools
And gangs competing to be the best.

Turf wars in this playground
Gasps of horrors by passers-by
The teachers need to clamp down
Gangs send their spies
To find out what the others are planning
All gangs advancing
Fist fights in the corridors
When will this horror end?

Jonathon Hawkins (12)
Burton Borough School, Newport

MY ODE TO YOU

Truth

Hey, come follow me to underneath the old oak tree.
That is what I want to say to you,
Every time I look at you,
It is hard to ignore you,
I try not to stare and hide,
But I'm falling to pieces inside.

Hey, look at that lovely blue sky.
But that is how I feel when I make eye contact with you.
My brain goes like jelly,
When I try to talk, my lips are stuck together.
The easiest thing for me to do is
Run, run, run away from you.

Atasha Gallagher (12)
Burton Borough School, Newport

THE TRUTH

Truth

T he home I live in is the home I love to stay in
H omes are places where the people I love can be found
E ven when I go home again it will only take a minute.

T rue love is the best kind to go around
R evealing my love would be so stressful
U seless telling you my love, because it would make me
worried.
T rue love is the best kind to go around
H elping me keep this secret wouldn't end up being
carried.

Beth Greenfield (12)
Burton Borough School, Newport

WAITING TO DIE

Dare

Taken away in the night
Left without a sight
Scared, alone
Waiting to die...

Electrocution, starvation, exhaustion
Overworked and underfed
Why Hitler? Why?
Waiting to die...

Vanishing one after another,
Striped pyjamas,
That's what they said,
What has the world come to?
Waiting to die...

Bombs blast in the night,
Oh they give me such a fright,
War over, I survived
Safe now...

Lottie Savage (12)
Burton Borough School, Newport

SECRETS

Truth

Sometimes they can be cruel,
Sometimes they can be kind,
They're kept unsaid,
Locked away
Deep,
Dark,
Unread,
Kept privately inside.
They're shared through giggles in the playground,
Whispered into ears at break,
Passed via limp paper notes in class,
But never told quite right,
For the real truth gets cast away,
Like those myths so long ago,
But the real truth is wrapped in mystery.
And no one will ever know...

Evie Wade (13)
Burton Borough School, Newport

DO WE REALLY WANT THIS?

Truth

S eas full of litter
A nimals fleeing jungles in fright
V irtually no more birds do twitter
E lephants push on with all their might.

T urtles stuck in plastic,
H urt and alone,
E veryone, this is drastic,

W e are messing up our home!
O ver-fishing causing empty reefs,
R ainforests are no more,
L ife is not for grief
D o we really want this?

Isabel Blasco (11)
Burton Borough School, Newport

DANCER OR WHAT?

Truth

You think I'm happy, well no I'm not
My legs, my hips and my back
Won't stop aching and aching
Won't it stop?

Yes I am a dancer, so what?

I dance every day,
Yes I know you might say stop!
But my heart is stuck,
In my song, in my dance,
Wait, there's no chance,
I won't stop I know I need to!

Physio, physio every week
My knees get weaker,
I can't even sleep.

Pyper Caitlyn Marshall (14)
Burton Borough School, Newport

MORE THAN MY BEST FRIEND

Truth

A horse gives you something that no one else can.
A best friend forever...
A partner in crime,
A friend as long as they will live,
Someone you can always trust,
Someone who will always love you.
People say it's just a horse,
It's a leader, a teacher and someone,
Who means more than anyone.
Horses are a part of me,
They made me who I am today.
A horse is more than just a horse...
A horse is my best friend.

Aoife Smith-Murphy (13)
Burton Borough School, Newport

STOP BULLYING

Dare

S o many people get bullied
T ry your best to help
O utrageous words are said
P eople can be so mean.

B ullying is a silly thing
U nless you've been bullied, you won't understand
L onely is how they feel
L et's make a change
Y ou can make a change
I nside they are hurt
N obody deserves to be bullied
G o ahead and help these people.

Jessica Louise Megson (11)
Burton Borough School, Newport

BEST FRIEND

Truth

For a wag of a tail,
And a bark of hello,
To no other friend
Would I ever go.
To whisper my fears,
He will lick away tears.
To run and to jump
And twirl all around
There is no better friend
That I have ever found.
He is your friend,
Your partner,
Your defender.
You are his life,
His love,
His leader.
He will be yours,
Faithful and true,
To the last beat
Of his heart.
Jasper.

Emily Sarah Fletcher (12)
Burton Borough School, Newport

LITTERING

Dare

Littering goes on and spreads and kills animals
It goes down to rivers, seas and oceans.
Please pick up litter
You could get fined a thousand pounds for littering.
Everyone stop littering.
Water animals could get killed,
By the carrier bags suffocating them,
Or even worse getting into their bellies.
You could also get a one-year jail term for littering.
Never litter, just wait for a bin.
Go and pick up your litter today!

Finlay Barber (11)
Burton Borough School, Newport

ZERO

Dare

When the world is gone...
Then will you care?
When you lose your job...
To the machine you made.
Then will you care?

Fires start to spread...
Disasters grow strong...
The world is ending
But you still don't care...

You throw litter on the ground.
Three...
You use your car to go down the street.
Two...
You live on your phone
One...
Look up, the world is gone
Zero...

Molly May Beacham (13)
Burton Borough School, Newport

INJUSTICE

Dare

Red shirts filled the stadium,
While excitement and nerves filled the air.
Fans began to cheer,
Little did they know disaster was near.

But!

Like sardines in a tight tin,
Everyone was packed in.
People began to be crushed,
Still though people pushed.

Many people died,
As others lied.
The fight for justice had begun,
The fight for the truth would not be fun.

Grace Seymour (12)
Burton Borough School, Newport

BOO!

Dare

On a cold frosty night,
The wind shuddered, 'Boo!'
The season is here,
Halloween night is to come.
With ghosts and frightenings one by one.
Trick or treaters bang on the doors,
The spooks come out with their claws
So the trick or treaters are running,
Running along the decrepit streets.
The Halloween spooks have won.
You've been caught!
So bid goodbye to everyone!

Megan Louise Harris (12)
Burton Borough School, Newport

MY UNCLE

Truth

My uncle was a great man,
He taught me how to fish
Like nobody else can.

My uncle was my best friend,
He became ill,
And was on the mend
But little did I know
His life was about to end.

It came to a day
When he was in hospital,
That day was definitely unforgettable.

I love my uncle
I cannot deny,
He is at rest now
Up in the sky.

Alfie Warren (13)
Burton Borough School, Newport

MEAN GIRLS

Truth

Mean girls laugh,
Mean girls cry,
Mean girls lie,
But most of all mean girls are mean!

They dress mean,
They act mean,
And they are mean.

Staring contests are the best
But not when you get beaten by the rest.

I make mistakes,
But they make them worse,
I spell things wrong,
But they make it worse.

Stop the mean girls.

Megan Elisabeth Suffell (13)
Burton Borough School, Newport

GRADING

Truth

Getting ready, putting the white uniform on;
The brown belt tied around my waist,
Stepping slowly into the huge hall.
Waiting and waiting for my name to be called,
Suddenly, I'm at the front performing a fight,
Again, I am waiting for everyone to finish,
Finally, I am at the desk, waiting for my grade.
I pass with a credit,
I run to the door and retrieve my brand new, uncreased belt.

Amy Pinto (13)
Burton Borough School, Newport

PURE PAIN

Dare

The dogs are howling
The cats are screeching
The mice are whimpering,
The rain is pouring,
So no one can hear.
All animals cowering
People stand above them towering.

All I can hear in my head,
As I lay down on my bed
As their fur is being shred
As animals are dying
As my tears of anger are drying
Are cries of terror,
Noises of pure pain.

Emily Jersey Clarke (11)
Burton Borough School, Newport

THIS WORLD

Dare

I'm trapped within this world,
The one with no escape,
Demons scream louder than your thoughts.
The darkness stalks him and gives no break.
He thinks how he got here,
Thirteen it seems.
If only people could hear,
His silent scream,
Why can't this just be a dream...
Wait weren't they supposed to love me?
Oh wait,
I can't be me...

Gaby Jackson (13)
Burton Borough School, Newport

WHAT ARE YOU FIGHTING FOR?

Dare

Everything is changing
Nothing is left
Another explosion, but what can it be?
Screams all around me.
Horror on every face
Gunshots mask all other noises
Only the ringing in my ears remains
I'm frozen still and alone
Terrorists everywhere
Shattering my heart into a thousand pieces
Crash!
They strike again
What are you fighting for?

Emily Paterson (13)
Burton Borough School, Newport

THE FOUR SEASONS

Dare

Spring falls in March and June,
But, the flowers rise oh so soon.

Summer rises in June and September.
But it's a season that we'll all remember.

Autumn comes in September and December,
But it kills the leaves on the trees.

Winter comes in December and ends in February.
But, we'll always be excited for the year ahead.

India Ellarby (12)
Burton Borough School, Newport

THINKING OF YOU

Truth

You left me, I was isolated.
I was lost in my own home.
I wait and wait; no call, no message
It's been four years now,
Since you left me alone.
My birthday, I blew out the candles,
Still waiting for your presence.
I'm getting older now; coming to my senses.
I realise that now you don't want me.
But in my heart I will always love you... Mum.

Alanis Gardner (13)
Burton Borough School, Newport

TECHNOLOGY IS EVERYWHERE

Truth

Technology, technology, everyone uses technology
Technology, technology, it is used in cytology
Technology, technology, it is used in geology
Technology, technology, it is used in mythology

Technology, technology, is always the best
Technology, technology, it will always lead to success
Technology can be used anywhere,
Even in the air.

Dominik Grebosz (13)
Burton Borough School, Newport

DEATH TO ALL

Dare

Never let the thought of death get inside your head
Death to come to us,
People suffering, dying,
Puffs of smoke released,
Animals, choking, killing, drained.
Factories working away
Grey skies above, taunting us.
Plastic floating,
They are choking.
Pollution kills, we all die, all of us.
Our graves are being made,
Escape...

Ellie Stevens (12)
Burton Borough School, Newport

FAVOURITISM IS UNFAIR

Truth

Favouritism is unfair,
It's in school everywhere,
Teachers choose their favourite student,
And forget the others,
Makes them wonder why they're hated,
So they need to change the way they are,
Don't you realise you have crushed their confidence to dust?
Not to glow or glitter,
But to make them cry and feel like litter.

Emily Malia (13)
Burton Borough School, Newport

HIDDEN

Truth

My hidden thoughts hide
Themselves.
How?
Lies.
I and others say:
'I'm fine'
Lies.
We all hurt inside.
'It's okay, not really!'
Lies!
'Don't worry'
Worry
'Stop, I'm fine.'
Keep going.
'Go away!'
Stay
'Go and find the light'
Go.

Abigail Richards (13)
Burton Borough School, Newport

UNTITLED

Truth

It waves and waves,
All night and day
It comes and goes,
But never leaves.

It gives and takes,
All night and day
It kills and births,
But never births child.

It is surrounded but yet surrounds
It makes war and peace
It makes warmth and cold.

It is the sea, a thing close to my heart.

James Lohan (13)
Burton Borough School, Newport

NATURAL REFLEXES

Truth

Happy, angry, sad
I think I'm going mad
Mother Nature's streams flow
In waterfalls they go.
While her plants bloom
She is crying in her room.
She sends tornadoes,
While people scream, 'No!'
But people fight back
Burning and ripping her map
Mother Nature imitates and mocks me
And hates me, does she?

Tyler Goodman (12)
Burton Borough School, Newport

THE OCEAN

Truth

There is a lot of commotion about the ocean,
About all the rubbish and trash,
Treasure that can be sold for cash,
Decreasing numbers of fish,
Because they are caught and sold,
And put in a dish!
Delicious
And whales being impaled by spears,
Sending people to tears,
Now their biggest fear
Is the ocean pollution!

Ethan Gatward (12)
Burton Borough School, Newport

OUR DEFORESTATION

Truth

What is going on today?
Is it just me and you?
It's a new dawn,
It's a new day
Now what shall we do?

Perhaps we should think of deforestation
And people dying of sleep deprivation
Earthquakes and whirlpools
They bring death and devastation
So we should really think about our deforestation.

Finlay Chetwood (12)
Burton Borough School, Newport

ENDING THE WORLD

Dare

L ittering is bad for the community

I t's awful for animals

T asting and dying

T reasured animals going down and down

E choing death after death

R eally wrecking the ocean animals' lives

I gnoring the signs

N ot going to stop

G oing to the end of the world.

Thomas Bratton (11)

Burton Borough School, Newport

TELLING THE TRUTH

Truth

Truth is the word that everyone hears.
I would never lie.
Remember that for years and years,
Even until you die.

What could happen if you tell a lie?
What about the consequences?
When you're telling the truth and passing by.
You should always have confidence.
Always tell the truth and never lie.

Eloise Cox (12)
Burton Borough School, Newport

EMOTIONS

Truth

Strong but then weak.
Happy but then sad.
Sometimes feeling hopeful.
Always dreading the bad.
Scared and uncertain
When will it end?
Embarrassed and mad,
Optimistic and threatened,
Block out the haters and you'll do fine.
You don't have to be mad
Because you're not the one in the bad.

Paris Skye Callaway (12)
Burton Borough School, Newport

WE

Dare

We are all the same,
We all breathe,
We all talk,
We all see,
We all have feelings,
We all walk on the same Earth.

We are all different
We think different
We talk different
We feel different
We cook different.

But we all have rights
And we are all the same.

Charlotte Holbrook (12)
Burton Borough School, Newport

FRIENDS

Truth

F ight for you

R espect you

I s there for you

E very time you need them the most

N ever give up on you

D efend you at all costs

S ave you when you are struggling.

Friends are one of the most important parts of *you!*

Gabriella Bickley (11)

Burton Borough School, Newport

LOVE LIFE!

Truth

Take risks
Live life until the end.
Treat others as you would like to be treated.
Try and achieve all your dreams.
Keep on dreaming.
Love life.

Make new friends
Keep your old ones.
Love your family.
Hatred is a strong word.
Talk to people and do not keep it in.
Love life.

Olivia Kessey (11)
Burton Borough School, Newport

FOOTBALL

Truth

Football games will give you quite a thrill,
In whatever weather, hot or chilled,
Making dreams become a reality,
Anywhere and everywhere,
Football is allowed for both genders,
Whether, you're a man or a female member,
Whatever shape, size, age or ability,
No one should ever become an invisibility.

Rebecca Gripton (13)
Burton Borough School, Newport

83

FIGHT

Dare

If there is one thing I've learned in life,
It's to fight.
Fight for what's right.
Fight for what you believe in,
What's important to you.
But most importantly,
Fight for the ones you love,
And never forget to tell them,
How much they mean to you,
Whilst they are still alive.

Prem Mehmi (11)
Burton Borough School, Newport

SPEED IS EVERYTHING

Truth

Got my new car,
Shiny as a star,
Ready for anything,
Speed is everything.

The speed is climbing,
Perfecting the timing,
Overtaking anything,
Speed is everything.

In the car of my dream,
Runs faster than streams,
Better than anything,
Speed is everything.

Morgan Groome (13)
Burton Borough School, Newport

THE TRUTH

Truth

I feel like a mouse
Trapped in a circle of sadness.
My heart is pounding so fast,
I am struggling to breathe.
The power to stand up to the bullies is trapped
Deep within; unable to escape amongst all the madness.
Finally, the courage unleashes
To confront the bullies who give in and leave.

Olivia May
Burton Borough School, Newport

THE SUN AND STARS

Truth

The sun is bright
And shines day and night
With the stars standing
By its side

It never sleeps
As it watches us

It binds our hearts as one
As the stars shine bright
Like the sun itself
For it is the eternal flame.

Louis Mansell (12)
Burton Borough School, Newport

IDENTITY

Dare

I am directed to be perfect,
Not expected to be me.
I cook you lunch and tea,
And I hate the way you look at me.

I put on a dress
Anything else would be a mess.
Why should I be stereotypical,
When I can be me,
And have my own identity?

Harriet Bailey (12)
Burton Borough School, Newport

THE LAST TREE

Truth

Trees getting destroyed,
Nothing is safe,
Birds squawking,
Hearing birds cry to their mother.
Animals go and hide to take cover.
Spending their last minute with their lover.
As they hear the cracking sound,
As the last tree falls to the ground.

Freya Cox (12)
Burton Borough School, Newport

WHY DO YOU JUDGE ME?

Dare

Words spill from your lips,
Words full of anger and rage,
Your hopes and dreams disappear,
This one word makes... the difference,
'She's too curvy'
'She's too fat!'
No! Stop!
You're just 'too' judgemental.

Stephanie Tomkinson (12)
Burton Borough School, Newport

WHAT HAVE WE DONE?

Dare

What have we done?
What we call civilisation,
The environment ruined,
Left in desperation,
What have we done?

Why?
Did every single creature die?
Not a single creature in sight,
Not even a tree, that thy eyes can see.
Why?

Connor Lewis (11)
Burton Borough School, Newport

HEARTS

Truth

How is the human heart so strong,
When it can shatter with a single glance
Or movement of the lips?
As your eyes become faucets
And a cracking is heard
Deep within.
As the strings of your love
Slowly connect
Only to be cut
Once more.

Amelia Reid-Mellor (13)
Burton Borough School, Newport

ANIMAL CRUELTY

Dare

A nimal cruelty must be stopped
N aturally we love our pets
I t must be dropped
M agic has not happened yet
A bandon cruelty
L ately we're horrible

Cruelty is naughty.
Please stop it now.

Chelsea Louise Davidson (11)

Burton Borough School, Newport

LOSING YOU

Truth

When I heard you were gone,
I felt like I lost my heart,
I felt I was gone,
I thought the world had ended.
Lonely, loving, it's all gone
It's lonely not having a laugh with you.
You will always be with me,
Wherever I am!

Molly Louise Leonard (13)
Burton Borough School, Newport

TURNING AND TWIRLING

Truth

Eyes tear-blinded
Down the path that led forever
Would it ever end?
For the life that I'd depend.

Life turning and swirling,
At times searching and lurching
Would the time come
How would I know?
Was it long ago?

Kelly Alice Griffiths (12)
Burton Borough School, Newport

WHY I LOVE FOOTBALL

Truth

F is for friends
O is for one love
O is for on the ball,
T is for good times
B is for best sport ever
A is for always doing it
L is for love it
L is for live it.

Emily Bullock (12)
Burton Borough School, Newport

PRISON

Truth

They shut the gates,
I walk in,
My time awaits,
I sit right in,
Bang! I put one foot down!
Boom! I kneel down!
Crack! I put my hands together!
Drip! A tear falls from my eyes!

Katie Jones (12)
Burton Borough School, Newport

EARTHQUAKE

Dare

Tall buildings shatter
Earthquake, earthquake,
The ground is shaking
Roads are battered
Earthquake, earthquake,
The world is breaking,
Houses are crumbling
Earthquake, earthquake,
The world is mumbling.

Taran Kang (12)
Burton Borough School, Newport

WHO?

Truth

The mystery,
About my identity,
The way you look at me,
The way they feel about me,
I'm just a girl,
No more hiding who I've always been,
This is me.
I'm anonymous?
No more...

Ruby Lily Gittins (12)
Burton Borough School, Newport

FAMILY

Truth

Always **F**orgive others
Respect one **A**nother
Makes you smile
In our heart
Laugh and share moments
Love **Y**ou

Tiah Summer Hunt (11)
Burton Borough School, Newport

BEACH

Truth

I love the beach,
Excitement for each,
The sand is yellow,
Like them weird Simpson fellows,
Fun for us all,
Just try not to fall
Because the salt goes in your mouth,
Tastes horrible like trout.

Kane Jones (12)
Burton Borough School, Newport

TSUNAMI

Dare

Whoosh, gone!
Is there anything left?
Destruction
Debris floating.
It's like a hand
Grabbing everything
Nothing would survive
This almighty fight.

Ben Yates-Ward (12)
Burton Borough School, Newport

A FISH'S LIFE

Dare

The fish came swimming,
As fast as they could.
I stay.
Dark clouds of blackness,
Are caving in on me.
Everyone is gone.
Soon I'll be next.

Kyle Richardson (11)
Burton Borough School, Newport

THE WELL-TRODDEN PATH

Dare

The night was hard, the night was dark
No stars did shine, no calls of lark
The demons came, the monsters watched,
A mother weeping, pressed to her child.

The day was tough, the day was hot.
No shade was there, their eyes bloodshot.
The vultures perched, the lions scanned,
The family together, hand in hand.

The dusk was long, the dusk was cold,
No child did speak, no stories told.
The bugs did bite, the sun did glare,
The embers glowed, the ash did stare.

The night was short, the night was brief,
The children wept, the knives unsheathed.
The soldiers screamed, their guns did point,
At the tiny baby, now lying dead.

The day was good, the day was bright,
The mother did cheer, no child did fight.
But the men came, fire in hand,
Burnt the fragile hut to the ground.

The air was still, but ashes blew,
No mother did cry, no child did spew.
A father walked, his child in hand,
Past the embers, alone on the land.

Harry Kite (13)

King Edward's School, Birmingham

VITILIGO

Dare

A single tear slides down my cheek,
Silently yet swiftly.
But that one tear means so many things,
It shows I can't keep this inside any more.

It's the little things like the quick glances,
The quiet murmurs or the subtle points.
Puzzled looks on the faces of people I don't know,
Or is it the quick movements when I go near?

Perhaps it's the bigger things,
The bigger colourless picture.
The taunting names like zebra, cow and giraffe,
Names that will haunt me forever.

And all because my skin is two colours not one,
It carves me,
Writes its story on my body,
It puts me down like a bully in a playground,
With help from strangers who can't hold themselves back,
It's the reason my eyes are turning red,
Whilst my skin is turning white.

My life is a puzzle just like my skin,
Perhaps I'm the jigsaw piece that doesn't fit in,
And no matter how hard people prod and poke I won't give in,

I won't break this mask,
Just to be how they want me to be,
I am who I am.

But sometimes I can't hold it all together any more,
I can't stay collected and calm,
And I cry and cry huge pools of tears,
I cry lakes and oceans of hot salty tears.

My heart pounds and so does my head,
People aren't aware of the mess that they make,
I just want to grab a megaphone and say,
So the whole world can hear,
It's called Vitiligo and you can't catch it.

It's where the skin pigment dies
It comes in all shapes and sizes,
On all types of skin.
Vitiligo doesn't discriminate,
It does not mind who will be its next victim.

It's hard to be different,
I'm different and no matter what people will say,
Call, shout and scream.
Nothing can take that away from me.

So next time you see someone different,
Don't stop to stare,
Just walk on by or say something nice,

If not it has a negative affect,
So if you stop to stare,
Point or say something to your friend,
Think about the person on the receiving end.

Eowyn Charman (12)
King's High School, Warwick

THE WATCHER

Truth

It was the day I was going to make a change to our country
The day I was going to get something right
I was going to be the hero.
And today was the night I would make things right.

Waved heavily goodbye to my family,
My love's tears trickled down from her eyes
I wanted to go back but I could not
Because today is the night I will make things right.

Suited up ready to go, then the nerves got me
Where do I go?
What if I don't return? Will they know?
But it doesn't matter because tonight is the night,
I will make things right.

'Shelter, shelter,'
What did they mean?
My hands clutched
And the air went tense.

Night fell upon me, the orange dusk came into my tent
The fright of getting killed comes to me again
1945, 1st October was the day I got killed
The night my life disappeared.

Aneeka Rai
King's High School, Warwick

THE FIRE THAT KILLED THEM ALL

Truth

In those dark early few hours,
The baker slept unaware,
That soon the city of London,
Would be burnt down from an unlikely flare.

Down on Pudding Lane,
The ovens were not raked out,
Though the baker seemed to think,
They were without a doubt.

The house made out of timber,
Soon turned to a roaring blaze,
And unfortunately for London,
There was no alarm to raise.

The inferno quickly spread,
Grabbing houses by the dozen,
The winds cheered on the fire,
While many cried to their mothers.

The flame swept through London,
Alighting anything in its sight,
Churches, houses, halls,

110

Families watched their homes,
Being engulfed by the blinding light.

For three days and two nights,
The fire decided to stay,
But the people of London were sick of it,
And wished it would go away!

Finally, the fire retreated,
Leaving six in their graves,
And London was at peace,
But the homes were still gone,
So they stayed flocked, as geese.

It is now a moment of history,
Frozen in various books,
But can we really imagine,
How they felt, watching their city in flames,
All thanks to a careless cook.

Christabel Alun-Jones

King's High School, Warwick

REVENGE

Truth

Once there lived a quiet young boy
All he would do is destroy
Angry he was all the time
His parents he would annoy.

His eyes fiery hot
A cold narrow smile
He got told off day by day
He had been like this a while.

Always in trouble at home
Up to no good in the street
Life on his own was quite tough
Teased by the boys he would meet.

On top of a bin at the side of the road
A dirty old match box he spied
He played with the matches for quite a long time
'Revenge is real,' he cried.

Across the road he spotted a shed
And there the match he threw
He watched as the wood began to glow
Into the fire it grew.

Anxiety started to grow in his eyes
As the flames spread quicker and quicker
The grass and the trees started to burn
And the smoke grew thicker and thicker.

People started to appear from all different houses
And then there was a big bang
The petrol can had exploded
And the sirens rang.

As the flames disappeared
He thought, what is this I've done?
I'll have to try and pay them back
I think I've learned my lesson.

Freya Richardson (11)
King's High School, Warwick

SEPARATED

Dare

I am too young says Mum.
I cannot understand?
You won't get it says Dad
I feel torn and twisted, separated between two.

Go with Mum,
Go with Dad,
But why?

I thought they were in love
Head over heels.
Nothing could come between them
An unbreakable bond.

But I was wrong.
So wrong I wasn't even aware
That they were fading
That something was wrong.

Oblivious to the world around me
The crumbling walls closing in
Suffocating me
Taking every last breath away.

You don't miss it until it's gone
You don't understand

It doesn't make sense
Until it happens to you.

And then your life changes.
The sun doesn't smile
The grass isn't green
When you're not sure how you feel.

Upset? Relieved?
Am I depressed or deflated?
All I know,
Is that I am lost.

Lost in my problems and mourning
Ashamed that I do not understand
Afraid of what's happening around me
Yearning that it's just a dream.

But it's not,
I am awake
And I am powerless.

Katie Burrows (14)
King's High School, Warwick

CONTROL

Dare

I am nowhere.
A different universe.
Alone, lost.
I have been here before.
I am helpless,
I am trapped.
Separated from all those I care about,
I'm unique, not like everybody else.
That's what they all say.
But different is good. Isn't it?
Or is it bad? I don't know anymore.
I'm too young, that's what my mother says.
To know who I am,
To know what I will be.
I just don't know.
I don't know anything.
No one seems to know who I am,
But do I know who anyone else is?
No one cares.
Not about me. Never
I need to go
Somewhere I can show who I am
Somewhere I can be me
I can't be me here

How do I leave?
Leave to my own world
To my painted reality behind my eyes
I'm gone
I'm drifting along the surface of the water
I jumped
In case you're wondering
Now I'm floating
Floating alone, by myself
Being unique
Unique is a good thing, I decided
An incredible feeling to be my own soul
A soul that can do anything
Anything it wants
Anything I want
I'm in control.

Evie Madeleine Griffin (13)

King's High School, Warwick

BLACK AT HEART

Dare

I am floating and turning,
Drifting away from this world
Feeling the wind, sun, earth,
Dancing over the edges of my face.
The bitter warmth; the icy wind,
Greet me as they melt into my timeless body.
I see an endless corridor
Meandering and twisting,
An infinity to an end.
Fragments of ideas, moulding together
A sea of hidden secrets; the mysterious hazed light.
Endless bubbles of thoughts, pieces
Fitting seamlessly into my dreamed puzzle.
The dew of the morning hangs still in the air,
The crisp chill gleaming in the light
Of burning, frozen stars.
I breathe in the intoxicating scent,
Of frost, pine and bark.
Riddling the aromas together
I flutter my eyes down, remembering
The memories I hold and I vow,
That I shall not, will not forget.
My inner drum quietens, as I sedate my breaths
As I keep dreaming, wishing, hoping,

DARE

In this concocted, fictitious reality.
Hearing the call of my name.
I find myself floating forwards, away,
Away from the tight safety net that stubbornly binds me.
That saves me from the truth; the hurt
The pain.

Shivanshi Bhatt (13)
King's High School, Warwick

MY BEST FRIEND

Truth

Have I picked you to love, to cherish,
To change the way I think?
Or have you chosen me?
To transform, to enlighten and
To push into a world of mystery?
I see a door that will suck me in,
Introduce me to a world of creation, imagination, my reality.
It is as though you are grabbing me by the hand,
Welcoming me,
Nudging me into a new land.
Is this a trap?
Will I ever be able to leave your tight grasp of my mind?
It feels as though I am floating, flying,
Sucked into a vortex, pulling me in.
I have arrived, I have met people, friends and enemies,
And I have travelled with them, I have seen monsters,
New and unknown places.
You have become my friend, altered the way I am
And introduced me to a whole new world!
This is all because you where there,
When my friends and family were not.
This is all because books are,
The quietest and most constant of friend.

Each friend I read welcomes me, sucks me in,
And teaches me about things I never knew!
Books introduce you and I to a world of
Creativity, blissfulness and a land
All of my own.

Hannah Broome (13)

King's High School, Warwick

WAR

Truth

Two pairs of eyes met,
They lit up like flames of a roaring fire,
Their hearts were pumping so fast they could explode,
A loud bang from the corner went off.

Thick black smoke covered the air,
Then another explosion,
A huge black shadow came from around the corner,
And pollution filled the air.

Screams deafen the ears,
People scattered around the city,
Red-hot sparks flew up in the air,
The other half of the city was stamping noisily.

Yelling angry people came from around the corner,
No one stood in their way,
Lying on the floor,
The mothers cried.

Fathers shouting,
Children running,
Homes destroyed,
The city in danger.

Silence fell,
The calming arrived,

People paused,
Realising what they had done.

Dark dawning morning arose,
Fires were put out,
Families came back together,
The city was rejoined once more.

People were playing happily,
Parents were cooking peacefully,
Mothers sharing cakes,
The city was one once more.

Megan Galliford (11)
King's High School, Warwick

BOMBED

Dare

I was there,
Lying in the trenches,
Silent,
Then a bomb hurtled from the sky,

Crash! It exploded noisily,
My whole body was shaking,
Coughing and spluttering,
I got to my feet,

The air was polluted with smoke,
Bodies bursting everywhere,
My lungs were burning,
I looked all around, no one,

Bodies were piled up everywhere,
Has everyone died?
I tried to scream,
But no sound came out,

I grabbed my gun,
Clenched my fist,
And started to march,
Inside my head everything was a blur,

It happened in seconds,
Where were my fellow soldiers?
Were they dead?
Why didn't I rescue them?

My feet were sore and blistered,
My body hurt,
But I kept on walking,
I didn't know where I was going,

So much was going on in my head,
Why did I decide to do this?
They said we'd be home by Christmas,
But we were not.

Qi Qi Xie (12)
King's High School, Warwick

UNDER THE BED

Truth

Stuck, on an island;
An island of safety and warmth
Layers of sheets and quilts
But nowhere to go

Things - very horrible, very evil, very hungry things
Hidden but ready to pounce
Where to go?

Monsters with obscure shapes:
Eleven arms, five eyes, a hundred teeth.
Starved for years.
The monsters are everywhere.

They're clawing at the edges
Trying to get out from under.

Some have claws as long and sharp as a knife
Others eyes were pools of black
A few with tails like whips
They had silver slippery skin
Filled with venom and poison.

You could smell the death lingering in the air,
Feel the hunger radiating across the room
Taste the metallic blood in your mouth
And hear the silent hisses bouncing off the walls.

Slowly more and more monsters could be seen
This was not an island of safety and warmth;
It was a jail of evil and desperation.

Anoushka Mundey (14)
King's High School, Warwick

LOST IN LONDON!

Dare

I've been lost,
Lost for days,
Scavenging for scraps in dark alleys,
Looking for familiar signs.
It's dark now,
The stars twinkle,
Mocking me from afar,
Reminding me of the family,
Of the friends, the opportunities that I've lost.
I must try, I must try,
These are the words
Circulating my entire system,
I can't get back, I can't get back,
Is what it is changing to.

I trod on through the alleyways,
Through the night,
Down narrow paths,
Between imposing, run-down houses,
There is no one to help,
No one to notice,
No one to comfort me.
I am alone,
I thought as I stopped walking, exhausted,

I am alone,
I thought as I lean against a wall, to go no further.
I am alone,
I thought as I collapsed like a rag doll
I am alone,
I thought as I breathed my last breath.

Anne Mynors
King's High School, Warwick

A PAINTING OF DEFORESTATION

Truth

Jumping into a tangle of dense vegetation.
My heart pounding through my body.
Adrenaline seeps through me,
Blending with excitement as it reaches my heart.
Looking up, I see a world of picture-perfect isolation.
An untouched world of astonishment.
Different creatures in all shades of the rainbow:
Swinging, climbing and scuttling.
On a canvas of green leaves.
I can hear their conversations,
Like splattered paint on a board:
They chatter, yell and scream.
I breathe in the fresh, clear,
Crisp air with the scent
Of secrecy on the breeze.
This is the painting every art collector
Longs to lay eyes on.
Then they came in their trucks,
They destroyed the world,
Tore down the canvas and
Wiped off the paint
Was this vision of perfection even real?

Now it is all gone.
A once beautiful painting in shreds on the floor.

Catherine Reynolds (13)
King's High School, Warwick

THE MYSTERY

Truth

I'm being turned, tossed and torn.
Infant hands grasp me like a fish being caught on a hook
Then being cast off like I'm not good enough.
Stuck in position till I get adjusted again.
Accessories being attached onto me one after the other.
One day a bearded builder
One day a tutu dancer
A top hat on my head
A tiara on my forehead.
My arms fall off then shoved on incorrectly
I'm just one of many manipulated models.
I gain and lose pets and friends,
Every day, hour, minute, second.
My ears burn from cacophonous children.
My heart pounds as fast as a child to food.
My body aches from being chucked around like a rag doll.
Wondering if I could ever have silence
Wondering if I could have calmness.
Wondering if I could ever have happiness.
It's a hard life being a Lego man!

Molly Charlotte McCusker (12)

King's High School, Warwick

MY FATE

Truth

I'm underwater, running low on air,
At fifty metres deep not enough air to get me to the top,
With only minutes left, I think of what I can do,
My air tank makes a noise, what shall I do?
I open my mouth to breathe,
Water flows through me, saltiness all around me,
The pressure of the water pulling me,
The water surrounding me, begging me,
Into its depth of nothingness,
I try to run away from my fate, but it's too late,
I can't take it anymore,
My mouth can't cope with holding me up,
Slowly, very slowly, I sink,
Into the deepest, darkest part of the ocean,
In every space the ocean could hear me, falling,
Failing to stay alive,
There was a thud and I hit the sand,
Misty clouds of sand floating upwards,
Begging me to float with them.

Gracie Lloyd (12)
King's High School, Warwick

NIGHT AND DAY

Truth

The dark, the dark,
How do you see?
It is bright brother,
What do you mean?

The moon rides high,
Up in the night sky,
Tonight, it is calm, tonight it is safe,
The moon rides high tonight.

Too bright, too bright
Why all this light?
Look sister,
Our animals thrive.

The sun sits high,
Up in the midday sky,
The days are kind, the days are fun,
The sun sits high today.

Dusk, dusk, the best time of day,
The night is coming soon
The moon will ride high
Into a dark, dark sky.

Dawn, dawn, a happy time,
The day is on its way,
The sun will rise and
Light the dark sky.

The moon, the sun,
Both powerful and strong
Both a light in the dark and yet,
Neither shall defeat the other.

Rachel Eslick (13)
King's High School, Warwick

I FEEL COLOUR

Truth

Life is a rainbow and everyone feels colours;
I feel...
Rage-red anger rising when my room needs to be tidied,
but in my eyes it's fine,
Cloudy grey hangs over me when life is dull
and the rain pours down outside.
Perfect pink blushes through me when the day is
perfect the way it should be,
Greedy green engulfs me when my stomach is empty.
Passionate-purple pulses through me
when I dance all my worries away,
Bare black shadows over me as I sleep until the day.
Neon-yellow lights me up when I share moments
with my friends,
Bitter blue embraces me when my homework never ends.
Warm white washes over me
when I feel calm and at peace,
My life is full of rainbows,
my feelings to release.

Amy Edwards (12)
King's High School, Warwick

UNTITLED

Dare

Trapped...
Drip, drip, drip,
Water trickles down my face,
A wave of sadness filling my heart...
My freedom is being torn away from me,
I'm scared, but I'm calm,
I'm alone, but I'm not...
The dripping turns to gushing,
My brain is overloading like an electrical fuse,
'It's going to be okay,' is what others say,
But I'm no fool, I know what's coming...
My heart is pounding, leaping out of my chest,
I'm trapped in a never-ending battle of freedom,
I turn to look at what my life has become,
When suddenly, time freezes and...
I begin to realise that I'm drowning in my own tears.

Freya Laycock (13)
King's High School, Warwick

RUNNING

Dare

I am running, running,
Running from death,
In the thick tall trees
Of a never-ending forest.
I want to stop, but I must not stop
Or it will catch me
Hurt me, tear me apart.

I am running, running,
Running from death,
But it never gives up.
It goes through
Goes under, goes over
Yet it always finds me.
I stop, my skin
Dripping with sweat.

I am not running, running,
Running from death,
And it has caught me
In its tight and painful grasp.
I cry for help,
But no one is there.
It swallows me...

Nathania Adu-Boahen (13)
King's High School, Warwick

A FRIEND IS FOR LIFE

Truth

Friendship, it's complicated
It's something money can't buy
No matter how much money you have
No matter how many things you own
A friend is worth more than anything.

The ups and downs on this never-ending roller coaster
When you fall out over something silly
When others get jealous of your friendship
If you can overcome these hurdles,
You will find the greatness of friendship within.

A fabulous friendship will be the final result
Never give up on a friend
They will always be worth it in the end!

Olivia Pascoe (12) & Gemma W (12)

King's High School, Warwick

LOST

Dare

I am walking,
I don't know where though,
Somewhere in the um...
In the wasteland.

The heat is deadly,
I need to find shade.
All around me I hear voices,
Calling me, reaching me,
They say, come home,
I miss you.
They shout my name.
Over and over.

The sun is setting and
The cold is caving in on me,
Capturing me.
No escape.

I can hear wolves,
At least I think they are wolves
I see it,
The light.
My family, friends,
Everyone, then...
Nothing.

Jemima Hunt (12)
King's High School, Warwick

TOO LATE

Dare

I feel light,
Like I've lost so much water - or I need to find more,
The sand under my feet no longer feels soft,
But spiky and itchy with a scorching hot blaze.
The day has been stretched I'm sure,
It feels like it will never get cooler,
Never stop harassing me.

At last,
The shimmering sight of...
No.
Yes!
Water...
I try to reach for it,
To feel the moist wet heaven,
But, as my hand stretches out,
The sky falls on me,
Creating nothing but a cave of darkness,
And I collapse.

Charlotte Emily Rachel Perry (12)

King's High School, Warwick

TREKKING

Dare

I am trekking, trekking, trekking,
Through the vast, unforgiving jungle,
It stretches over the horizon every way I look;
It draws me in further until I am completely lost,
An array of plants and wildlife surround me,
Like a botanical wall,
I can hear the fluttering of the breeze,
The sighing of the wind,
And then,
I hear a noise,
That nearly makes my heart stop beating,
A sinister snarl from hidden depths,
The distinctive noise clutched at my heart,
And made me think of only one animal,
A tiger!

Millie Perkins
King's High School, Warwick

WORLD WARS

Dare

Man, woman
Deeply in love,
Always together,
Never alone.

Countries at war,
Horrifying days,
Men were summoned,
To take place.

Lover gone,
Falls to her knees,
Prayers said,
Shed a tear.

Silenced by sights,
Thousands down,
Scattered at his feet,
Like autumn leaves dropping down.

A single shot,
Bullet through the head,
Slumped down,
Joining all around.

Evie Jeavons
King's High School, Warwick

HOMELESS

Dare

I woke up startled,
My heart pounding like lightning,
I've got no money, no home,
Only a rusty street bench,
The rain is hitting me like bullets,
As the dark clouds,
Want to cave in on me,
Distressed people looking out at me,
The colourless street,
The people walking past me,
Starving, wondering what's going to happen?
I can feel my fate closing in on me,
I try to run,
But it's too late.

Olivia Smith (12)
King's High School, Warwick

ALONE

Dare

Alone, alone, alone,
She is always there even when I am not,
Her words haunt me forever,
Inside I hurt like I am being stabbed,
My heart cries for help,
My mouth is numb,
My body drowns in desolation,
When I speak my words escape me,
I am trapped in fear,
A deadly, never-ending nightmare,
Fragile, weak, sorrowed pain,
Alone, alone, alone.

Maddy Phillips (12)
King's High School, Warwick

145

HURRICANE IRMA

Truth

Heartlessly exterminating
Silently seizing
Its petty preys.

Sweetly sinfully,
Seizing,
Suffocating,
Smothering,
Its frameless figure.

Girl, boy, man and woman
Satisfying its infinite,
Starvation.

Blood, sweat and tears
Its work is finished here.

Thuwaraha Viveananthan (13)
King's High School, Warwick

RISE OF JUDGEMENT

Dare

Day of judgement, not for wonders,
You will be scared forever,
Be ready to surrender,
Louder than a billion thunders.

This will be the world's worst thing ever,
Buildings falling over people,
Even more painful than stepping on quadrillion needles,
This will destroy all of the world's treasure.

Horrors way past your imagination,
Killing people, you are the witness,
The god breaks all boundaries, with his mightiness,
This will shock the whole nation,

This is a situation that you can't avoid,
Thinking you were the best,
But you are the worst,
This will get you annoyed.

Everything would be destroyed,
There is nothing left,
Now you are really stressed,
This is even worse than an impact of million asteroids.

Mudassar Hussain (12)
Kings Heath Boys' School, Kings Heath

YOU

Dare

There are no two people the same.
Everybody is free to be who they wish
Whether you believe in God, Allah or Buddha
Whether you are Pakistani, Korean or English.

If only all people thought the same way
That all should be treated like the other.
This rule should apply to every single person.
Your friend, your enemy, your mother.

Some people say they support LGBT
Others say that it is unnatural
The truth is people feel this way
Like it or not, it is not supernatural.

Some people say it is a sign from God
They say some people will go to Hell
A certain book says everybody is bound together by God
Does this book ring a bell?

No matter what you believe or feel
Somebody is always going to believe differently and
disagree.
The only person whose opinion matters is yours
Nobody can stop you from being yourself, trust me.

I know who I am
Not all people have that privilege
People are abused and forced into depression because of
this
In this world, that is an unacceptable image.

People shouldn't be criticised for being themselves
Your mind is constantly refreshing and becoming a new
Whether you are black, Chinese or gay
Consider every single person,
Or they won't consider me and you.

There are no two people the same.
Everybody is free to be who they wish
Whether you believe in God, Allah or Buddha
Whether you are Pakistani, Korean or English.

Harry Cleaver (12)
Kings Heath Boys' School, Kings Heath

UNITY

Truth

Unity cannot be taught,
But it is learned.
It cannot be bought
And it should not be churned.

Unity is not based on singularity.
It is based on trust.
Like trust
It is hard-gained but easily lost
Like a house of cards,
It only takes a little...

To have unity is not,
To make everything the same,
To unwittingly copy what was taught.
Unity is the combination,
Of everything that makes us unique
Of everything that separates us.

Deny unity
And you are a fool.
Do what they say
And you are a tool.
Carry their weight
And you are a mule.

Belief provides unity.
It can be broken as easy as a twig.
But nurture it,
And you will find
That the obstacles that once stopped you
Are broken by those who support you.

Fight against oppression and greed
And you will find that you have been freed
By the weight that is being borne
By those who want unity.

Yousef Atallah (16)
Kings Heath Boys' School, Kings Heath

NATURE

Dare

We all think nature is eternal,
Just like corn having kernels.
It never starts, it never ends,
But it always amends.

We all think trees are eternally ample,
At the rate we're going, trees will tremble.
Without trees life will become incomplete,
And someday from Earth we'll have to retreat.

We should recycle whenever we can,
And make the most of what we have.
Without trees there will be no air
And the world will have none to spare.

Stop. Think about the future generations,
Provide them with a strong foundation.
Stop and think about global warming
Be the one to start reforming.

Muhammad Ali Gohir (12)
Kings Heath Boys' School, Kings Heath

RONIN

Dare

My other half continues to walk
Gently stroking his red-tailed hawk
While I stay behind to catch my breath
I make a small prayer encouraging my death
We left the nest in too much haste
Just for a chance to get a taste
Of what the world had to show
Now all I know is it felt like a blow
I caught his eye, green as jade
And as sharp as his blade
He was kind yet cruel
And as tough as a jewel
Which is why when he fell
I knew I was in hell.
The hawk landed on my shoulder
In my weak state he had the weight of a boulder
And I realised that, as I stroked his hawk,
That I was the only half who continued to walk.

Muhammad Swara (14)
Kings Heath Boys' School, Kings Heath

YOUNG WRITERS
INFORMATION

We hope you have enjoyed reading this book – and
that you will continue to in the coming years.

If you're a young writer who enjoys reading and creative
writing, or the parent of an enthusiastic poet or story writer,
do visit our website **www.youngwriters.co.uk**. Here you will
find free competitions, workshops and games, as well as
recommended reads, a poetry glossary and our blog.

If you would like to order further copies of this book,
or any of our other titles, then please give us
a call or visit **www.youngwriters.co.uk**.

Young Writers
Remus House
Coltsfoot Drive
Peterborough
PE2 9BF
(01733) 890066
info@youngwriters.co.uk